July's Christmas Doll

Dakota Christmases Remembered

by

Robert W. Feragen

for Dick and Cynthia

Robert W. Feragen

All Rights Reserved © 2013 by Robert W. Feragen

This 2013 collection is a fourth printing. Previous issues with the title *Dakota Christmases Remembered* were produced by the author using a computer printer and hand binding the pages. This publication has been renamed to match the cover art and adds the story "The Last Christmas" to the earlier published five stories.

The cover illustration is the work of John Green, an artist noted for his wildlife paintings which are marketed through the John Green Studios, Madison, South Dakota.

ISBN 13: 978-1482650662
10: 1482650665

In memory of my parents
Helen Frances White Feragen
and Thor Feragen
who gave their children many gifts,
among them the joy of family Christmases

Table of Contents

Forward..vii

Homeward at Christmas..ix

A Special Christmas Edition.....................................1

July's Christmas Doll..15

Two Trees for a White Christmas..........................27

A Dumb Christmas Wish.......................................45

A Child is Born for Christmas...............................57

The Last Christmas..69

Foreword

The Great Depression of the 1930s taught children old enough to understand that there were many dimensions to an economy of scarcity. I am sure that we children at that time did not get the entire sense of our parents' worries – the long nights they must have spent wondering what to do once they had lost their home and business. But despite their cares they succeeded in instilling in the children of my family a spirit of wellbeing. They helped us to understand that what we had in material things was sufficient, at least for the time being.

At the beginning of the Twenty-first Century it may be impossible for those who did not experience the "dirty thirties" to realize that we did not have huge shopping malls with stores devoted entirely to selling toys. We did have a big department store, Shriver-Johnson's in downtown Sioux Falls, where Christmas displays and the sound of Christmas music held at least one boy enthralled by the season.

Christmas for a child in 1938 was as exciting and filled with anticipation as that for any child today who may be expecting a newer and more powerful electronic game. Our expectations then about the number of gifts which we might find under the tree were modest– limited to the hoped for one, possibly two toys. We knew that other gifts would be "useful" ones, such as socks, underwear, or a new shirt. But the lights on our Christmas trees were just as bright, the songs just as nostalgic, and the candle light in church just as magical as they may be for any child today. The truth of the matter is that our family loved the Christmas season.

In these few stories I have attempted to catch the spirit of our family's and our Dakota community's celebration of that holiday. These stories were written as a kind of meditation upon my family during those times. They are fictionalized accounts of actual events in which I use a storyteller's bag of tricks in the hope of extracting larger meanings from our experiences.

The introductory poem was written some years ago for our family's Christmas card. A revised version is included here to set the mood for what follows. The story "July's Christmas Doll" was published in the July/August, 2000, issue of the *South Dakota Magazine,* and the story "A Special Christmas Edition" was published in the same magazine in its November/December, 2002, issue.

The cover illustration for this collection was used as the cover of the July/August 2000 issue of the *South Dakota Magazine* and is used here with the permission of the artist John Green, Madison, South Dakota, and the magazine whose editorial offices are in Yankton, South Dakota. My sincerest thanks to John and the editors/publishers Bernie and Myrna Hunhoff.

Homeward at Christmastide

Homeward we bring our hearts at Christmastide,
Drawn by a winter eve's warming light,
Where family and friends linger at our side
And a darken season is turning bright

We gather within the assuring scent of pine,
Ourselves and this home made evergreen.
Holiday lights and eyes of children shine,
Protected by household nisser seldom seen.

This season of giving provides all we desire,
Our reward of family the priceless gift.
Cherish ever those days when children conspire
In toy-bright worlds free of war's fearful rift.

Come, celebrate this season of innocent birth
And miraculous grace showered upon the earth.

[Nisser are elves in Norwegian mythology who protect the household when treated well by the family. To keep in the good graces of the nisser it is obligatory for a family to put out a bowl of *rømmegrøt* (sour cream porridge) with a big *smørøye* (eye of butter) in the center of it on Christmas Eve.]

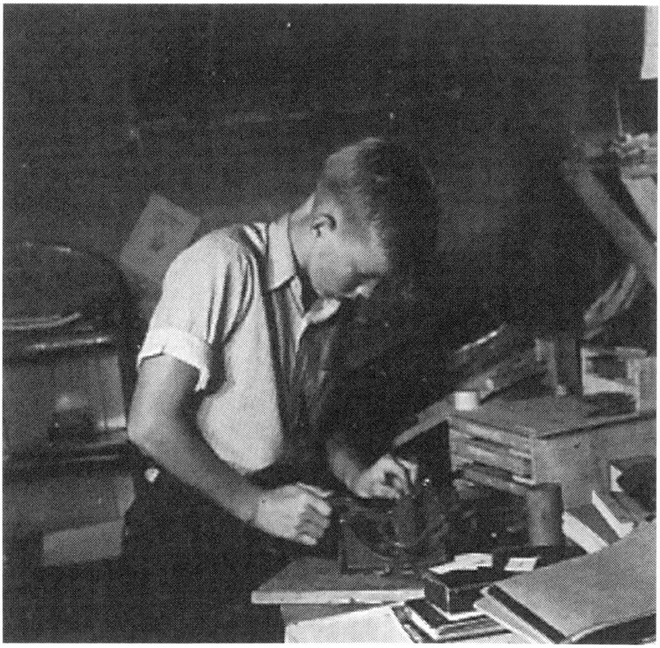

A Special Christmas Edition

Johannes Gutenberg and Swede the tramp printer were my heroes in 1937 when I was twelve years old. Christmas of that year my parents rewarded my interest in printing by giving me my first printing press. It was a Kelsey 3x5, hand-powered press that used real lead type just like that used to print the Dell Rapids Tribune where Swede worked as the journeyman printer. I was learning some of the tricks of the trade which Swede would show me, like driving a wedge of a wood match stick into a line of type to tighten it when regular spaces would not fit. Those bits of learned skill began to certify in my own mind that I was becoming a member of that brotherhood of craftsmen who reached back nearly five hundred years. Of course, I knew then that I was going to be a printer's devil for a long time. There was much to learn of the trade and of the lives of printers like Swede.

Christmas morning in 1937 I found the little press under the tree, its gray metal paint so new one could smell it among the medley of holiday odors. Even after sixty years the invigorating smell of pine trees suggests to me gifts with a hint of freshly painted metal. A red ribbon had been stuck to the round ink plate at the top of the press. My name was boldly printed on a tag. All around this longed-for gift were packages wrapped like other presents but containing fonts of lead type, a small type case, and The Instruction Book for Boy Printers.

It was the week before that memorable Christmas morning that I learned a lot about printers. On Wednesday before the final printing on Thursday of the Tribune's Special Christmas Edition, Swede presided over a print shop disaster. In contrast to today's world of four-color graphics on the front pages of even weekly newspapers of small circulation, or the micro-second, flashing images streaming across a television screen, the Tribune of that day would appear to be a very drab publication. If you were to go to the local library archives to inspect the weekly newspapers of that era, you would see they had been printed from old, time worn type, the letters not very sharp. One's impression would likely be that those publications were quaint, if not merely crude. But the surface appearance of a newspaper of those days, as in surface appearances in much of life, fails to convey the essential human story that lay behind the tedious effort to produce them. I was witness to that furious effort during the hectic week and the crisis that cursed the last hours of getting out the special Christmas edition.

A regular edition of the weekly Tribune would have four to six pages, but the special edition would add another four pages. The newspaper was printed two pages at a time on the flat-bed press in the basement with its huge rotating cylinder taking the sheets down across the oscillating bed of inked type. Each of the two pages was made up of hundreds of pieces of lead type, columns of linotype slugs, and illustrations called "cuts" mounted on wood blocks, all of which was wedged into a heavy cast iron frame. These pages were assembled in the upstairs shop on a huge stone-covered table, called the imposing stone. When all the pieces were put together in the frame, called a chase, Swede then would begin to tighten the wedges on two sides. To make sure everything was tight, he would lift a corner of the chase and push on the face of type to make sure it was not loose and pull out of the form when inked in the press. The tension in the chase was tremendous, but necessary to hold all the parts together.

It was Christmas vacation and I was allowed in the back shop to talk to Swede and to watch the final steps of putting together the "greetings" page of the special edition. This was the extra money-maker for the paper because almost every business and professional person in town bought an ad wishing the readers holiday happiness and prosperity in the coming year.

Swede was intent upon his job and under pressure because of the extra pages to be printed. I sensed that anxiety and didn't ask him a lot of dumb questions about what he was doing. Swede's life history wasn't something he talked about much. I didn't know if he had kids of his own, or a wife. He had told me he'd worked on newspapers in Wisconsin, Iowa and Minnesota before coming to the Tribune, not explaining why he moved a lot. Mr. Sibley, the editor and publisher, had explained to me that men like

Swede were called "tramp printers" because they moved from place to place, taking on work as they needed it.

"Most of them are pretty skilled workmen, but when they get itchy feet, nothing will keep them," he explained. He didn't tell me what caused the itchy feet.

It must have been four o'clock in the afternoon when Swede was locking up the final two pages of the special edition. He'd tighten the wedges, called quoins, along the two sides of the chase, and then with a maple block and mallet tapped over the entire surface of the page of type to make sure every piece was the same height for printing. Then, after more tightening of the wedges and testing to make sure all parts were holding, Swede tipped the heavy frame on edge in preparation for carrying it to a dumb-waiter elevator that would lower the form to the basement and the big press.

Two newspaper-sized pages of lead type and linotype slugs are heavy, weighing a hundred pounds or more. In his fifties, Swede was lean and muscular and prided himself in being able to handle just this kind of heavy lifting. It was with ease then that he picked up the double-page form and turned to step over to the elevator. I was standing on the other side of the imposing table and saw the explosion of type spew out of the frame and onto the floor. The clatter and heavy thump upon the floor was sickening, even to me who had done none of the work. Hours of tedious assembly lay in a pitiful heap of metal and wood on the oiled floor of that shop.

There was no movement by or word from Swede for a full, deathly minute. He stood over the mess, the empty chase still in his hands. Without a word he dropped the iron frame onto the floor with the rest of the disaster, stepped over the pile and walked out through the front office and into the street.

What could a twelve year old do? I went around the table and got down on my knees before the pile of metal. I thought maybe I could pick up some of the bigger pieces. Before I had touched any part of the destroyed pages, Mr. Sibley came to look down at the heart of the special Christmas edition.

"No need to touch anything," he said with resignation.

"There won't be a special edition this year?" I asked.

"Oh, I think so. Swede will be back later after he's settled his mind at Charlie's Bar."

I wasn't sure I believed Mr. Sibley. On the way home for supper I walked down Main Street to see if I could look inside the barroom where Mr. Sibley said Swede had gone. The door to Charlie's was plate glass through which I could see that the dimly lit interior had festoons of Christmas lights strung from wall to wall. Neon beer signs flashed on and off. It seemed a dark and fearful place to my eyes, strangely celebrating a holiday of peace on earth. Several men on high stools were leaning on the bar, their hands around tall glasses in front of them. I thought I saw Swede at the far end of the bar, but I could not be sure. It was not a place where a boy was welcome.

My walk home was through a mild December evening where heaps of shoveled snow from weeks before had become dirt covered. With a week to go before Christmas the gray stained landscape reflected our weariness with the season. We wished for a fresh snowfall, for a perfect white Christmas. My mood was as dim as the neighborhood until I entered our home. The smell of mince-meat pie was sweet on the air, and the evening meal was beginning to be laid out on the dining room table by sisters Ellie and May, assisted by my youngest sister Beth. My brother Richard was reading in the living room. Although Dad was on the road this week, making his usual calls on merchants in small towns all across eastern South Dakota, we expected him home on Friday.

My home was warm and brightly lit but I could not get from my mind the image of one lonely tramp printer sitting in Charlie's bar. I wondered if he ever had a home like ours. I wondered where he would spend Christmas day. Then, remembering what Mr. Sibley said, I feared I might never see Swede again, that he would get itchy feet tonight and drift off to another struggling weekly paper to ply his trade, leaving the disaster at the Tribune for others to put to rights.

All Thursday morning I hesitated to go to the Tribune office to see if Swede was still there, fearing that he had left Dell Rapids for another place. Mother must have caught my solemn mood, for she asked, "Aren't you going down to fold papers today? It's Thursday, you know."

"Yeah. I know."

"Well, don't mope around here all day. Mr. Swede is probably waiting for you to help."

Encouraged, I finished lunch quickly and ran to the newspaper office. I hoped that the big press would be pounding away for the final printing. As on every Thursday all hands would be folding the papers ready for mailing. I went around to the alley and the basement entrance to the pressroom. The sounds of the press operating could be heard up the alley, a happy sound to my ears on that day.

When I opened the door and went into the basement the familiar swish of ink rollers over the type form met my ears. The cylinder was rolling across the form as a double page sheet was printed and lifted onto a pile at the end of the press. Double page sheets fluttered like wings of an angel as they settled onto other printed sheets.

Swede stood on the raised platform of the press feeding sheet after sheet to the cylinder as it rotated. Clamps caught the edge of a sheet and held it to the cylinder as it rolled over the double page of inked type. I could see that it was the special greetings pages that were being finished. Swede smiled down on me from his perch.

"Kinda late, aren't you," he shouted over the noise of the machine.

"Yeah," I said. "I'm sorry."

And I was sorry, sorry that I had doubted Swede would finish his job.

Among the presents under the tree on Christmas morning was a small one-inch cube wrapped in red paper. It was heavy for such a small package.

"Your friend Swede dropped this by for you after I told him what you were getting for Christmas."

When I opened the little package I found a solid lead cut of soldiers in the uniform of the American Revolution. It was that night that I produced the title page of "History of the World," printed over that drawing of brave soldiers. Swede knew I would need it for important work.

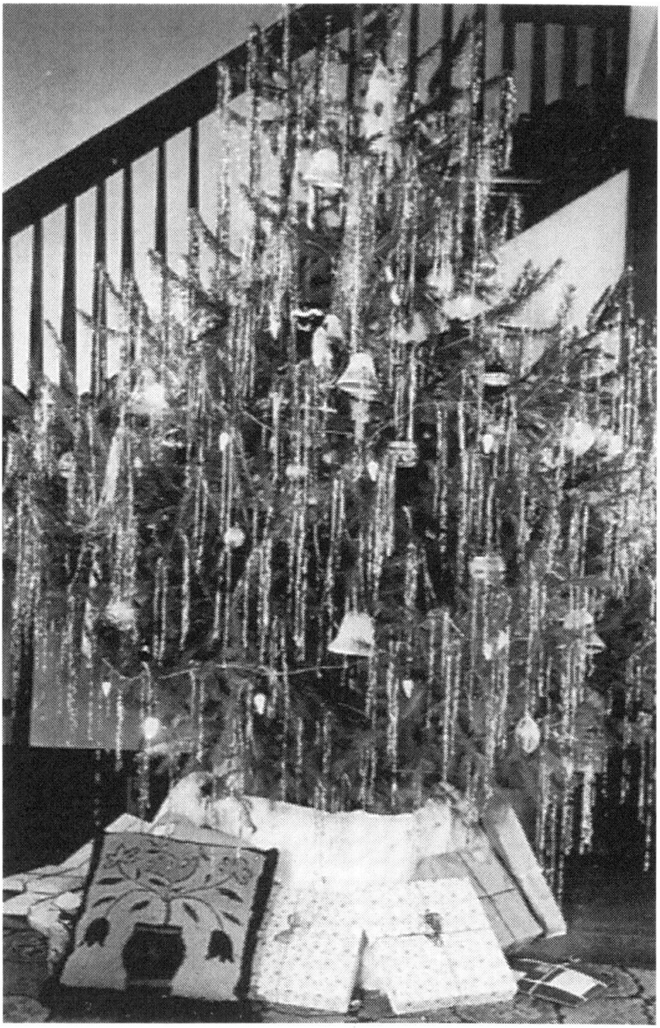

July's Christmas Doll

The sky-darkening dust storms which swept in from the west were like bad omens the year we moved to South Dakota. There were no signs that the Great Depression would soon change for the better. My father had lost his business in North Dakota but with good luck had gotten a job as a traveling salesman for a mercantile house out of Chicago. All we had was hope.

There were six of us children. I was number five. The two oldest, May and Margaret, were already in high school. Ellie and I were in grade school and Beth wasn't yet five. It was a family of two worlds: that of the older children who remembered family prosperity in North Dakota, and we three younger ones who recalled little about the good life then.

My brother Richard and I shared a bedroom. He was seventeen and had begun to shave. At Christmastime, when the kids began to be careful of each other's feelings, he would be friendly and tell me about that distant time when my father owned a big store.

Richard told me about going on hunting trips with Dad. They went up country on the North Dakota prairies where men and teenage boys sat around a campfire to talk about the grouse and prairie chickens taken that day. He described for me the camp smells he remembered–the scrub oak fires, the canvas tents, Dad's pipe. I wished with all my heart that I could have lived in that time.

In the middle of July soon after my ninth birthday, Dad invited me on a trip with him.

"How'd you like to go on the road for a few days?"

It was an exciting idea. We weren't going hunting, but I was going to be alone with my Dad on a trip. I hadn't expected the invitation because in those years he was often gruff about more worries. He wasn't always like that. He enjoyed Christmas. He led the march down the stairs on Christmas morning, with Beth, the youngest, holding on to his hand as the rest of us followed in order of our age. And when his spirits were high after the presents were all opened he would sing songs from the Old Country. He would tell us about the *nisse*, those magical little people that watched over the farmstead and brought good luck.

On the day before the trip, while I was preparing to leave, Mother said to me, "You must try to help your dad all you can. It will be as if you're a salesman like him."

Mother sounded as if she had won another argument with Dad, of having bargained for something that was deserved but hard won.

Beth didn't like being left out, crying, "I want to go too. I want to go with Daddy."

"We'll just let the men go on their trip," Mother said, "and I'll take you to a movie downtown."

Mother and I packed the musty paper suitcase she had found in the basement. She lined it with newspapers and counted out socks and underwear for three days. A worn but carefully pressed clean shirt was folded and placed in my suitcase.

"Dad's going way out to the Missouri River," she told me. "You're big enough now to help carry sample cases for him."

As Dad drove us west out of Sioux Falls I thought about going back to school that fall and being able to report on my trip to the Missouri River. At the beginning of classes, teachers would ask us to write about what we had done during our summer vacations. There were always some kids who reported going to Yellowstone Park or to a lake in Northern Minnesota, but some of us didn't have vacation trips. All that week as Dad made his calls at stores in little towns, I memorized their names so I could report on where I had been, towns with names like Epiphany, Montrose, Emery, Kimball, Mitchell and Chamberlain on the river.

That first day we continued west with the car windows rolled down for a breeze. Already at ten o'clock in the morning the temperature was in the high 80's. The air had a lingering taste of dust. This adventure into my father's world began with his mood light. He bragged to me about his driving skills.

"Just watch the speedometer. It won't move off fifty whether we're going up hill or down. Steady driving. That's what makes a car last."

By noon I was hungry and Dad kidded me about not getting along without having food every ten minutes. Then he told about hiking in Norway.

"We'd hike over a mountain with just a little pack on our back and go for two days with just a piece of cheese and a small loaf of bread."

He adventured for me in mountain country as we rode down gravel roads, dust billowing after us in the scorching sun on that wide Dakota prairie. We both longed for the cool pine forests of Norway that day.

"It must be nearly one hundred," he said as we drove slowly into a small town whose main street was the same gravel road we'd been following for half an hour. Some of the store windows were empty and had farm auction bills taped on the inside. We would eat, he said, after he'd made his call on the Ben Franklin store.

"Can you bring in case number two?" he asked, pointing to the back seat on my side.

When he got out of the car the thin plastic pillow he used to support his back during the long hours on the road had stuck to his shirt. I laughed at him from the car.

"Are you going to wear that pillow, Dad?"

"You were going let me go in there with that thing hanging on my back, weren't you?" he chided me in mock reprimand.

In the stifling heat of the dusty street we were sharing a joke. He was a proud man, but he could still laugh at himself. It was as if our banter of understanding bridged the canyons between the good days and these with so many worries. I pulled the sample case from the back seat with the confidence of an experienced traveler. I followed my father into the Ben Franklin store.

"Here's a nickel," he said when we got inside, continuing our confidence.

"Don't tell your mother about candy before lunch."

He nodded toward the candy counter to the left. He took the case and went to the back of the store, and was greeted by its owner as someone known for years. They talked weather, burned-out crops.

Mrs. Gridley worked in the store with her husband. A large woman, she had a generous smile for the young son of the salesman from Sioux Falls.

"You're Dad's helper today," she said. "Does he pay you real good?"

She spoke loud enough for my father to hear. From the back of the store Dad said something about my just learning the ropes. It was not a large store and I could hear the men talk as I pointed out to Mrs. Gridley which penny candy I wanted for my nickel.

The sample case was open and my father held before him a baby girl doll with a pink frilly dress and bonnet. He was saying that July was not too early to order Christmas stock. He spoke earnestly, describing the credit arrangements to Mr. Gridley, who said nothing. Father offered an alternative order, something that would not mean as much money. Mr. Gridley replied that times were tough. Father suggested that money could not be made without having the right stock. The doll would be a popular item.

The men talked earnestly, respectfully. Mr. Gridley did not resist the sales talk. He deferred to my father while Dad laid out the reasons that by Christmas the economy was going to get better. Father had removed his straw hat and wiped his brow as Gridley spoke in a soft voice about the trade area thereabouts and how sales had not been going well.

When my father lifted the doll from the sample case once again, showing Mr. Gridley the careful way in which the dress had been made and talking about value, I knew he needed help. He was not persuading Mr. Gridley. My father was losing the sale. This would be a useless stop and our trip would end up as another "bad" week.

I stepped forward and looked Mr. Gridley in the eye.

"If you don't buy that doll you're a dumb nut," I blurted out.

In all the years since then I have never known the depth of silence that followed my outburst, not on dark nights of desert war, or vigils for my own ill children. The quiet in the store may have lasted seconds or minutes. I cannot by any means available to memory measure the time during which both men looked down at me, their expressions as alike and frozen as two statues in church.

In the next fraction of a moment I was rushed outside the store. The sidewalk was searing hot in the noontime sun. My father's grip on my left arm was unrelieved. He was speechless except to repeat two or three times, "Inside the car. Inside the car." He thrust me forward and I crawled onto the baked interior of the Chevrolet. I watched him retreat into the store in his shirtsleeves. The entire back of his shirt was wet with sweat, his thin hair awry from exertion.

That moment, that snapshot of memory of his entering the door of the Ben Franklin store stays fixed and unaltered in my memory. It was his retreat from my loyalty. He was caught there in that doorway, in that store with the Christmas doll and I could not help him. I can never know what those two men said to each other after that scene, but years of living have taught me that they both were playing their parts, both understanding the dignity each had to preserve.

On the road again, dust rising under the car and behind us as we left town, my father drove in silence. I stared out at the shriveled and parched cornfields, at the blown soil reaching up into fence lines. Through the open car window the July Dakota wind burned into my eyes for an hour of desperate silence.

Then he said, with an incomparable grace learned in that season of depression, "Don't worry son. It's okay."

Mother wanted to know how the trip went. I told her that I got to stay in a hotel room with Dad. Otherwise, it wasn't so special.

***

Two Trees for a White Christmas

The rituals of Christmas in our family during the 1930s seemed to be as carved in stone as the laws Moses brought down from Mt. Sinai. Just as my Dad and we six kids expected Mom to prepare turkey for Christmas dinner, with all the "fixings," Mother and the rest of us expected Dad to bring home the perfect tree to be decorated on Christmas Eve.

Our Christmas tree had to be perfect in every way: at least eight feet tall, the needles sound and not already shedding, and the conical shape unmarred by vacant areas. After all, the tree was the center of our celebration of a timeless ritual. The sight of bright lights on the tree, the smell of evergreens in the house, and the excitement engendered by brightly wrapped presents were all a core part of our family life. The tree and the presents under it would mark the fulfillment of the year letting us begin anew.

Photographs in the family album of decorated Christmas trees record the march of time, a note in the white margin of each black and white print telling the year we had that particular tree. This photographic record testified that our evergreens had been up to the serious glory of the occasion. The inflexible nature of this standard of excellence was maintained by Mother and was made especially clear on the day before Christmas, 1938, when I was thirteen.

Since it was Christmas vacation I had been at the schoolyard with my friends. We had been sliding down the one hilly street which the town blocked off just for sledding. As it got dark at about five- thirty and having been warned not to be late for supper, I ran the two blocks home. It had begun to snow big flakes that drifted down through the warm light from inside the houses I passed. Lighted wreaths in some of the windows glowed brightly, their twinkling lights reflected on the blanket of fresh snow.

When I got to our front porch, my brother Richard, who was five years older than I and home from college for the holidays, was sitting on the top step, his Mackinaw jacket buttoned tight against the wind that was beginning to stir from the north. It was strange to see him sitting there when dinner should be ready and on the table inside.

"Mom's crying," was all he said as I approached.

"What'd you mean?" It was hard for me to believe that mother was crying because she seldom cried. She met adversity with a steely silence and inward resolve which hard experience of lean years had honed to a fine edge.

"She's mad at Dad because of the scrawny tree he brought home tonight. Have you seen it yet?"

"No," I answered. "I've been sliding over to the blocked off street."

"It's inside. Dad hasn't put it in the tub of water yet. He's explaining to Mom."

"Explaining?" I asked.

"He said it was the last one on the lot. He was sorry, but he had driven all the way from Chamberlain today and got in town late. Couldn't be helped. None of the tree lots had much of anything left."

Richard was thinking what to do but wasn't ready to let me in on it, not for a few minutes anyway. I wanted to go in to eat but he told me to stay out of the house. Dad was still explaining, he said again, and that Mom was saying Dad should have tried harder because Christmas was only once a year. Rich thought dinner was going to be late, a major catastrophe in my opinion.

"So how come you're sitting out here?" I asked, knowing the answer – when Mom was crying and Dad was trying to explain, we kids were just in the way.

"I'm thinking I know where there are some nice Christmas trees," Rich said.

"Yeah?" I challenged. "If Dad said the lots are all out of trees, what makes you think you can find one?"

"I was just remembering when I worked on Dubois Farms near Hartford two years ago. Bunch of us high school kids were hired to pull weeds out of a lettuce patch. I seem to remember they had trees growing there too. A tree farm. Maybe they've got some that haven't been cut."

"So what?" I was getting too hungry to struggle with a complicated problem.

"Wanta go in my ol' Lizzy and get us a good Christmas tree?"

Lizzy was what Rich called his Model T.

Richard was like my Dad. When he made up his mind, he was like a bulldozer plowing through snowdrifts, pushing everything aside. When he got that way, he and Dad sometimes had words. It kind of scared me when they argued.

"I'm going to tell them we're going to hunt for a tree," Richard said finally, getting up from the steps.

In two minutes he was out of the house again.

"What did Dad say?" I asked.

"I think he gave up explaining anything to Mom. He said if I was so darned smart to go ahead. But I don't think he's very happy about our going."

Rich argued with Dad a lot, so I guessed that tonight was like other nights. Rich was going to do what he wanted even if he showed up Dad for not trying hard enough. It was as if Rich was going to prove he could do what our Dad couldn't do. But I went along. I sure didn't want to go in the house just then.

The Model T Rich bought last summer when he was working in the Dells quarry to get in shape for college football didn't have a heater. I was cold when I got in old Lizzy and got colder as the frigid air seeped through its loose doors and windows. My mittens weren't much good for keeping my hands warm, being wet from sledding. My legs were cold too, but I didn't dare say anything. Rich would just call me a sissy.

The snow was coming down harder as we headed out on the country road west of town. It was one of those back roads that didn't get plowed very often.

"What if we get stuck?" I said, making it sound as if it were going to be a fact, not a possibility.

"Come on. Quit worrying. It's only about a couple miles to where we turn south. They wind will push us all the way to

Dubois's. Besides, I got chains for old Lizzy. We won't get stuck."

It kind of scared me the way Rich said that. It sounded to me that he expected he'd have to put the chains on in order to make it home.

The wind was blowing snow snakes across the road ahead of us in the dim headlights. I was glad there were no drifts over the road yet, even if the northwest wind was blowing hard across the road. The countryside shone a pale light from the snow-covered fields. Farmhouses were far apart. As we passed one farm we saw a man carrying a milk pail and walking head down against the wind. He was kicking his way through drifts to a tiny white house nearly invisible in the blowing snow.

After we had driven for thirty minutes, Rich could see that I was getting worried. I thought he was too because the wind kept getting stronger and he hadn't said anything.

"Don't worry," he finally said. "We got only a couple miles to go. Right after we turn at the next corner. Besides, aren't you glad we're really going to have a white Christmas."

"Yeah," I said, not too sure what all that snow was going to mean for us tonight.

I guessed Rich knew what he was doing. He was like that - always confident and able to get things done. He was kind of like a second dad to me, being much older, so I knew he'd take care of us in the storm. Although we swerved in icy ruts a couple times, the wind was really pushing us along with the blowing snow. I worried that we would have to drive straight into the wind on the way back.

"Won't be long. Right over this next hill," Rich said, finally.

He was right, of course. There was the sign at the section corner. "Dubois Farms, Henry and Helen Dubois, Proprietors. Fresh vegetables, poultry." The sign said nothing about trees. That worried me, but Rich was sure they grew Christmas trees too.

We drove right up to the back of the farmhouse out of the direct wind. Snow was swirling around the corners of the house, eddying into sculptures under the faintly lighted windows. Rich left the engine running, afraid that it might be hard to start again.

"Stick with the car," he shouted in the wind as he got out. "I'll go ask,"

Rich ran to the back door, his head turned away from where the snow curled around the house. I watched as the back door opened and a big man filled the frame. I couldn't hear what they were saying, but in a minute Mr. Dubois had his coat and cap on and came out near Lizzy. He was pointing.

"You can take one of them out at the end of that row there. You'll see where some were already cut this year."

"How much for a tree?" Rich asked.

"Well, seeings how you're going to cut it down yerself, two dollars will do."

Rich pulled bills from his pocket, paid Mr. Dubois. Taking an ax from the back seat of Lizzy, Rich ran over to the dozen trees along a fence line. I could see him through the blowing snow, running back and forth. Then he stopped. I couldn't see the tree very well, but I knew he had made his decision. He began to chop hard and fast. It must have been really cold out there because it was sure cold in the old Model T that seemed to shutter as much as I was.

Pulling what looked like a wide branched pine behind him, at least eight or nine feet in length, he pushed through the snow to the car. Rich opened the back door of Lizzy, tossed the ax onto the floor and retrieved some rope. Snow swirled into the back seat. He tied the tree to the running board on my side, its trunk pointing forward like a ramrod. In the light coming from the house windows I could see that Rich's face was bright red. Mr. Dubois stood stamping his feet as he watched my brother.

When Rich had the tree tied tight, Mr. Dubois shouted at him, asking if he had chains for the car.

"Sure do," Rich shouted back.

"Well, I'll help you put them on. It's going to be a rough twenty miles back to Dells. You better get over to US 77 to go home. Little longer way but if you get stuck, you'll more likely get help there."

They jacked up the back wheels, put on chains on one, then the other tire.

Rich jumped in the car, cupping his hands and blowing on them. He was shivering now too.

"Whew," was all he said at first. Then we heard Mr. Dubois shouting through the wind.

"Merry Christmas, boys. Be careful."

We both waved to him through the front window, yelling "Merry Christmas."

"A beauty. It's really a beauty," Rich said as he drove Lizzy slowly down the driveway to the road. He turned away from the way we came, explaining that it was the way to the main highway. It was slow going because we were going east and the wind hit us on the left side, shaking the old car. Sometimes we had to stop until Rich could see better when there was a let up in the wind. I thought he was getting a little scared when drifts began to form across the road. They weren't very big at first, just five or six inches deep in the center of the road. But they were getting bigger as we crawled along, bumping over one, then another. The old car rumbled as the chain-wrapped tires rolled over the frozen gravel road.

"Sure glad Mr. Dubois helped me with the chains," Rich said as we plowed through another wind-packed snowdrift. "He remembered me from working for him."

Rich's voice sounded a little hoarse. I guessed he was worried now about getting through to 77. We didn't talk much after that but both of us stared into the unending cascade of snowflakes blowing across the road. The light from the headlights reflected off the wall of blowing snow. We could hardly see ten feet in front of us.

About then he said, "I'm kinda scared."

I waited for him to explain, but he didn't say anything.

"About getting stuck?" I asked, finally.

"No. About Dad. We gotta figure some way not to show him up."

"How we going to do that?"

"I don't know yet. But you gotta help me."

It took almost an hour to get home. We could see the faint glow of the town's lights at first before we saw anything we recognized. Then there was Morgan's Garage at the end of the bridge over the Sioux River. Down Main Street we drove, the diminished wind in town sending eddies of snow around the ends of buildings as if to beckoning us on. When we turned on to our own street, all the houses looked warm and safe. The storm now seemed like nothing at all, even if the wind was still strong.

Rich untied the tree from the fender of Lizzy. Holding it upright, he marched up onto the front porch in triumph.

"Open the door," he shouted to me over the wind.

I did as he said and stood aside as he tipped the tree through the front door and paraded it into the front hall. I watched the hero's welcome. At first Mother scolded Richard for going out in the storm, and at the same time was saying what a beautiful tree he had found. Dad was smiling a tired little smile. Then he clapped Richard on the shoulder, saying, "Well, you did it."

Then I watched Dad go into the living room and fill his pipe and pick up a newspaper. He had backed away from the jubilation going on in the front hall where

Rich and my sister Ellie were putting the stand on the new tree as Mother watched. I couldn't be sure then, but have imagined since, that Dad was feeling both pride and hurt. He knew he had capable sons. But he had been put aside for a few hours. I remember feeling kind of sad.

Rich had told me what I had to do when we got home. I figured it was time to get rid of the scrawny old tree that had been stood in the corner of the entryway near the front door. I took it out onto the front porch and down the steps. In front of the barren spirea bushes was a four-foot high pile of snow where we had shoveled the walk during the past week. This is where Rich told me to put the scrawny old tree.

The wind was still blowing and adding more snow to an already white Christmas Eve. I pushed the tree trunk into the snow bank and turned the side with few branches against the bushes. The good side faced toward the street. That pitiful tree, I thought, would at least stand like a welcome to our Christmas celebration.

Richard had gone to the basement to get an extension chord. It didn't take us five minutes to put a single string of blue lights around that scrubby tree.

"Go in and get Dad," Rich said.

I nearly pulled Dad out of his chair and led him by the hand out the front door. Mother followed us onto the porch. Dad stood inspecting his lighted tree, his pipe in his hand. He didn't say anything at first, and then laughing said, "Looks like we'll have twice the Christmas cheer this year."

Mom was crying again!

A Dumb Christmas Wish

Being a new kid in a small town is full of risks. There are trials to be gone through, challenges coming from the oblique for which a thirteen year old can hardly prepare. As in much of life, people sometimes show a veneer of good will, of feigned friendship, that masks malicious intent. One's softer side becomes exposed to easy attack. So it was for me in the Christmas season of 1938 when the family moved to Dell Rapids, South Dakota.

The best way for a young boy to get acquainted in town, my mother was convinced, was for him to be involved in activities. School clubs and scouting were her favorites while my instincts were to sit on the sidelines and see how the land lay.

"Bruce," Mother said, "you have to learn to mix with the other children."

Mother prevailed, of course, and I was signed up for Boy Scouts by mid-November, just weeks after we had moved to town. Plopped down in a new classroom in the middle of a semester was challenging enough; reporting to the first troop meeting with my only uniform a brand new scout bandana around my neck was in boyhood terms just short of terrifying. I knew that the other members of the troop, some of them in my class at school, were waiting for my first stupid move. They waited for the foreigner to stumble and, in their eyes, do some dumb thing. They knew it would happen but I didn't.

The Great Depression, lingering in its effects well into the second Roosevelt administration, caused my father to continually seek cheaper house rent for his family of five kids, wife and one grandparent. So it was that we moved from time to time. This latest move was from what had become for me a familiar city neighborhood in Sioux Falls to what seemed at first a sullen, rural

Dell Rapids twenty miles away. Those first weeks in school went by without incident, except for Rodney Skalt telling me that Diane Monfort was his girl friend and to stay away from her. Diane was the prettiest girl in the seventh grade and certainly the one that was most interesting to me. Rodney must have noticed. But Diane hadn't noticed. In any event, I was too shy in those early days of school to have approached her, so Rodney had no need to worry.

The week before Christmas vacation was relaxed in the classroom. In our art period we decorated the windows with wreathes cut from green construction paper. Our teacher had brought a small evergreen tree into the room, which we decorated with colorful chains made of paper. There was great excitement when we exchanged names for the gift exchange planned for the Friday afternoon party. Although there was a lot of guessing about who got whose name, the name we drew was to be kept secret and the wrapped gift put under the tree without the giver being identified. The idea was that this anonymity of gift giving, of "silent generosity" as our teacher put it, would surely launch us into the spirit of Christmas.

Despite Rodney's threat, I had secretly hoped to draw Diane's name but in fact got Rodney's. That is the way fate sometimes works, I have since discovered, and is not to be questioned too closely. Buying a present for Rodney within the dollar limit our teacher had set was a challenge to which I might have given more thought, since I didn't really know him very well. A toy of some kind might have been a wiser choice, but with my literal mind deep in the school setting, I thought the brightly-painted, wooden pencil box would not only be handy, but it was rather unusual. Rodney didn't think so when he ripped off the red and green Christmas wrapping and held up the box for all to see. He commented loudly, "Looks just like Bruce's caliber." Everyone laughed. I did too, even if I wasn't too sure what "caliber" meant. But it was enough of a judgment to make me blush in fear that everyone knew that I had given him that off-beat gift.

Friday was the last day of school before Christmas vacation. It was also the day on which our scout troop was to distribute food baskets to the poor on the south side of town. Class Christmas parties were scheduled from two-thirty to three-thirty in the afternoon with dismissal half an hour early to accommodate other activities.

Our scoutmaster, a rotund and gruff father of one of the scouts whom I knew only as Fish, had organized the food boxes with the help of other parents. He was waiting with his farm truck for eight of us at the school entrance. There was room for all of us and the boxes of food in the truck bed. We hung on to the high wooden slats of the truck sides as Fish's dad drove slowly down the street and through brightly lighted downtown. Snow was piled along the curbs from past weeks of storms. On that early evening, the sun was just going down and the darkening sky beginning to show blinking stars though the frigid air.

The truck crawled down what were for me unfamiliar, unpaved streets at the tag end of town. The adults knew which houses where to get boxes, the criterion for selection a mystery which had not been shared with us. Our task was to carry a box to what in most cases were houses not much finer than shacks, some with boarded-up windows where glass had been too expensive to replace.

As we rumbled into the neighborhood, there was much laughter among the scouts. The brisk, cold air invigorated our spirits. Each of us got to take a box up to a house alone. We were instructed to say "Merry Christmas from Boy Scout Troop 23."

Fish came back from his delivery saying that there were three young kids with their mother waiting for the food box.

"They looked really happy," Fish said.

Rodney said sarcastically, "Yeah, I bet," which seemed strange to me. I guessed that he hadn't got the Christmas spirit yet.

I was given a box to take up to a little white house where a single light shone through the front window. There was no response to my knock at first. I was beginning to get cold as I stood there waiting because the wind had come up and was blowing snow down the rutted street.

The door opened. A stooped old woman, her gray hair pulled back into a bun, stood in the dim light. I could see that her face was deeply wrinkled, which made it seem to me she was frowning. But as I was about to hand her the heavy box of canned goods, flour, and bread, she asked me to come in and put it on the table.

The smell of cabbage was strong inside, but there was also a musty, suffocating odor of some salve or medication which made me catch my breath. I think I was afraid being in there, but I managed to say "Merry Christmas from Boy Scout Troop 23" as I went to the kitchen table.

The old woman's wrinkled face was turned up to the single light overhead and was beaming with a broad smile. She had no teeth and her words were slurred as she said "Oh thank you, sonny. Thank you and God bless you." She patted my left hand as I put down the box. I think I said "You're welcome" as I hurried back out into the frigid, clean Dakota air.

It had been the first time anyone had thanked me like that. It was strange and somehow wonderful feeling, but I was uncertain about my feelings. I wanted to get out of that house even if I was happy to have taken the box to the old woman.

A house or two later it was Rodney's turn to take a box to a house. He came back to the truck on the run, clambering up over the tailgate of the truck.

"Jeeze," he exclaimed," what a dump. Stinks like everything."

Some of the scouts laughed at what he said, but some of us didn't think he had the Christmas spirit yet.

Then, out of the recesses of my mind, out of that uncritical reservoir of feelings that often fails to get said just right, I blurted out, "I wish strangers would bring me gifts tonight."

Rodney howled. "You dummy," he shouted. "My dad said they're a bunch of dead beats. That's why they're poor. You want to be like them?"

He pushed me or I pushed him first. I can't remember. Two of the others were laughing with Rodney as he pointed at me and began to chant, "Brucie wants to be on welfare. Brucie wants to be poor."

I jumped off the back of the truck and ran to a clump of trees and bushes. Fish's dad didn't know I'd jumped from the truck and continued to drive down the street.

It was never clear to me what was said on the truck after I ran away. The truck didn't come back down the street to look for me. It wouldn't have mattered because I was crouched behind a thicket of bushes which was filled with snow. The wind continued to blow snow into my face and chilled my whole body as I hid motionless in the winter's night. I could think of nothing to do but phone my parents and ask for a ride home.

The old woman's house was a block back from where I'd jumped from the truck, and I ran there as much as to get warm as to reach my parents quickly. Again there was a long wait for the old woman to answer my knocking on her door. She was surprised to find the same boy standing at her door, this time empty handed and confused.

"Can I use you telephone to call my parents?" I asked.

"Oh, sonny. I don't have a telephone."

"Oh," I replied lamely.

"You come in here, though. You look a fright."

She took hold of my left arm and almost pulled me into the close, fragrant heat of the room.

"Now I'm going to heat you a cup of tea to warm up. It must be below freezing out there."

I don't remember saying much more than "Thank you." I watched that old person move about her kitchen, stooped and slow, and I wondered about all the years she had lived. There was nothing but an aura of the ordinary about her, but her toothless smile was assuring. I couldn't explain what happened. I just said I wanted to get home right then, before the scouts were finished.

She must have guessed there had been some kind of argument and that I had lost. She sensed that I needed a friend just then because she said, "It was real friendly for you to bring me a Christmas box. It's just like the gifts strangers brought to the babe in the manger."

When it was time to leave I buttoned my jacket tight to my chin, wrapped my scarf around my neck and pulled my stocking cap down over my eyebrows. I said "thank you" again as I was about to open the front door and run toward town.

"Merry Christmas, son," the old woman said. "May your life be blessed."

What I said in the truck had been a dumb wish. When I grew wiser I realized that the half hour in the old woman's home let me see that the poorest among us can have dignity in the face of the casual generosity of strangers. It was the dignity and grace of that old woman which were gifts to wish for at Christmas.

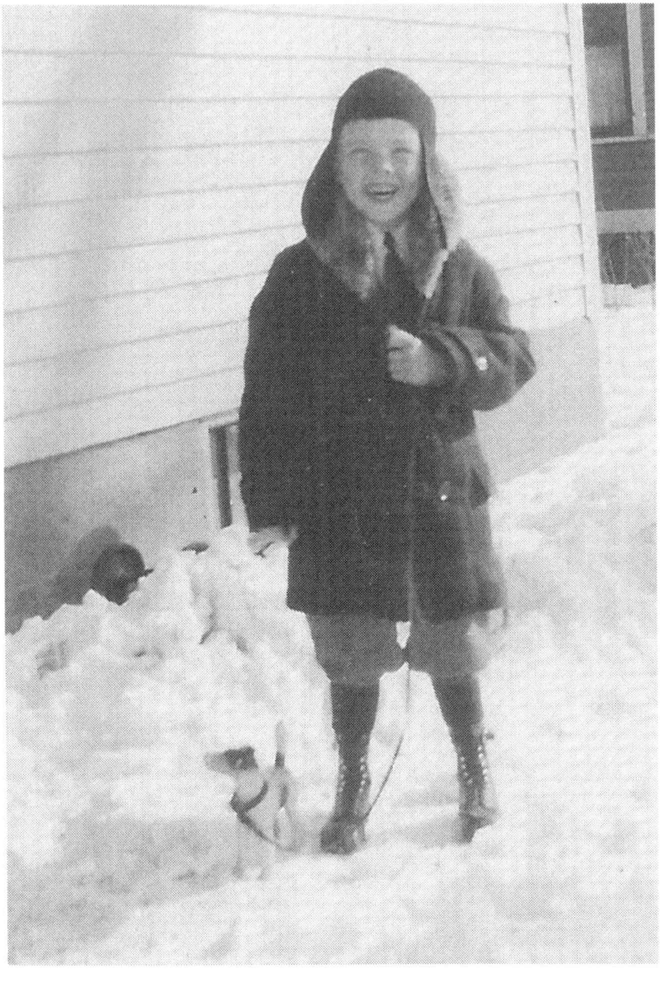

A Child Is Born for Christmas

Memories from early childhood are often like the images of a kaleidoscope, slowly turning, falling into place, then changing, one colorful fragment following another. A tattered, old fashioned Santa Claus Christmas card before me brings to mind the Christmas a month before my fifth birthday. It is a Christmas that looms brightly in memory, dimming any recall of earlier such celebrations.

The foreground memory of that Christmas was of my being deposed as "baby of the family." Sister Beth had been born in May of that year. The event changed my self-centered and pampered universe. A lesson was embedded in what was to me a mysterious and complex series of events – the family's solicitous concern for a swollen mother and then her returning from the hospital with a ruddy creature all bundled in pink blankets. The babe attracted a great deal of interest. My four and a half year old mind was willing to accept these mysteries as given, maybe even ordinary because they were accepted by all in the family as part of the order of our world. What I had not anticipated was that this helpless baby would usurp my privileged reign on Christmas morning.

The holiday season in our home meant weeks of mounting excitement. Packages were wrapped in private with tantalizing hints dropped casually at the dinner table. Cautions were expressed by our parents about "not wanting too much" because of the "times being hard." The stock market had crashed, Father's retail business was suffering, the serious extent of which I would not understand until years later. That gift-giving would not be as generous as in previous years, was expressed obliquely by Mother when she remind all of us that we were to be thankful for the many gifts we had already. Such gentle hints cast a cloud over my anticipation of toys in abundance to be found under the tree Christmas morning.

Our family's excitement reached a peak at dinner on Christmas eve. There were speculations about whether Santa Claus would be able to get around to all the homes on this particular night because of the bitter cold. Temperatures in North Dakota were nearly twenty below. None of us dared to venture out of the house. After eating supper we lingered at the dining room table to listen to Dad tell us about Christmases in Norway where he grew up until coming to America at eighteen years of age. He described how his family would celebrate for two weeks, right up to Epiphany on January Sixth. He said his family would take sleigh rides to the homes of relatives or neighbor's for overnight visits. That seemed strange to us because the only relatives in town were our grandparents who lived next door. Dad said that sometime his whole family would ski to the neighbors, maybe a mile or two away. His description of the evergreen covered hills of Norway, snow-covered and shimmering in the moonlight, painted an enticing picture of a faraway, magical place. I could imagine the dark mountains he described rising up from the forests, their peaks snow covered. In the high crevices would be the lairs of fearful trolls, who threatened Billy Goat Gruff in Dad's story.

But, Dad assured us, there were good elves too. The *nesser* were little people who watched over homes and farmsteads during the year. They had to be rewarded, Dad explained, or bad things could happen, like a cow getting out through a pasture gate that had somehow been opened. He told how children put out bowls of rømmegrot for the *nisser* on Christmas eve to reward them. The treat would keep the elves happy, although they might still decide to play tricks just to remind the household from time to time not to forget them. That was the reason, Dad said, a thimble or small cup might be lost and never found again. The *nisser* had hidden them away..

At the time I thought my brother Richard, who was then twelve years old, was like a *nesse*. He wasn't short but he was full of tricks and practical jokes, setting traps into which I would fall with a happy smile in those early days of my life. He short-sheeted my bed once after returning from YMCA camp where he learned the trick.

Richard and I shared a room, being the two boys in the family. There he was commander in chief. His dresser drawers were out of bounds, never to be invaded, or even opened a crack by a curious sibling. I accepted his rules, recognizing the persuasive power of his greater age and strength. And I looked up to him because he would read to me at bedtime, and tell me stories about his adventures on the Mouse River in Minot, North Dakota. Ours was a comfortable relationship. But Richard would make up stories, I discoverd as I grew older, as he did that Christmas Eve.

"Do we have a *nisse* to protect our house?" I asked Dad as he told the story again.

"Well, I suppose we do. But I've never seen one," Dad replied.

"I have," Rich said, and everyone laughed.

"But, we haven't put out anything for them," I reminded everyone.

"Well," Mother prompted, she who had not lived in Norway and whose family came from Illinois, and before that, New England, "in America we put out cookies for Santa Claus. And tonight, Bruce, you and I will certainly do that. We wouldn't want Santa to miss Beth's first Christmas."

The reminder that Beth was to have Christmas with the rest of us was the only sour note on Christmas Eve, but I soon forgot it as Mother handed me a plate of cookies for Santa. It was the duty of the baby of the family to put the plate of cookies near the front door because we didn't have a fireplace. Since Beth was only eight months old, it was still my job on this Christmas Eve. With that ceremony done, it was off to bed for Richard, Ellie and me. Ellie was three years older than I, and still not old enough to be in or decorating the Christmas tree with our parents. Margaret was and she and my parents would stay up late to get the tree ready with the presents arranged under its boughs.

"That is the way it is done in the old country," Dad told us.

We were all warned not to sneak downstairs to peak at the tree or it would disappear and not be there in the morning. So it was to our rooms with the doors closed. Our excitement was too great to allow us to get to sleep right away. Richard started to read a story to me. After awhile he suddenly stopped and listened very carefully. He crept out of bed and crawled over to the double windows that looked out at our front yard.

"Brucie. Don't make any noise," he whispered hoarsely. "Come here to the window, quick."

Rich spoke with alarm, as if something was wrong outside.

I got down on the floor and crawled to where he knelt at the double window facing the street. He held back the curtains and had his face close to the glass. His breath spread a mist over its surface. On the storm windows frost had formed over the lower half, making delicate patterns of leaf-like shapes.

"What's wrong, Richie?" I whispered.

"Look up there," he said, pointing high into the sky past the bare tree limbs of the elm that stood in our front yard. "Do you see them?"

"See what?" I whined.

"The tiny reindeer. If you listen carefully you can just hear the harness bells ringing. Jingle, jingle," he whispered softly.

The moon was low in the sky. Ice crystals drifted on the still air, glistening in the faint moonlight. No living thing was moving in our neighborhood. There was no wind. And in the deep stillness, I could hear the distant tinkle of bells. Far above us, it seemed, a wisp of shapes curved through the sky, shapes of tiny reindeer, as certain as the late hour.

"See them now?" Rich asked.

"Yeah. I can. I hear the bells, too. I can just barely hear the bells."

"That means Santa will come to our house tonight," Rich assured me, as he stood up and went to his bed.

"But you better get into bed," he added, speaking aloud and no longer whispering, "and go to sleep or Santa will be frightened away."

I hurried and got into bed. But I did not understand his saying that Santa could be frightened by me, or my family. But it was not the time to take a chance.

In the dark of our room, the frosted windows faintly glowing in the moonlight, I was caught in the magic of this season of gifts, warm under blankets and protected from the bitter cold. I didn't dare say a word but I knew that Santa had come to Minot, North Dakota. I wondered how Richie could fall asleep so quickly.

My Father loved Christmas and the excitement of his children. Christmas morning he was up before any of us were awake. He went down into the frigid basement to stoke the coal-burning furnace so the house would be warm for us. Then, before coming back upstairs to our bedrooms, he would crank the Gramaphone and put on a record of Christmas music.

By the time Dad got back upstairs, all of us were lined up at the head of the stairs which went down into the front hallway just off the living room. The tradition was that the youngest in the family would lead the procession, privileged to be the first to see the dazzling tree that morning. It was my place at the head of the line. But, with Beth wrapped in a blanket in his arms, Dad stepped in front of me at the head of the stairs. He turned to the rest of us and said, "This year we have our own new Christmas child." With that he started down. I was in second place.

The dazzling surprise of that year's Christmas tree was dimmed for me for a few moments as we followed Dad across the hallway and into the living room. There, reaching to the ceiling and crowned with a crystal spire, was our tree, all ablaze with lights, tinsel and sparkling ornaments.

"Now, before we open gifts, Bruce gets to see what Santa left him on the cookie plate," Mother said.

I ran to the front door where I found the plate I had left there the night before. On the plate was a Christmas card with a big picture of Santa. I took the card to Mother to read to me. She opened the card with solemn ceremony, as if something very important was about to be read.

"Dear Bruce," Mother read, "Christmas is a birthday. It celebrates the day a child was born. And this Christmas a child has been given to your family. Beth is precious, just as you are precious, and Ellie and Richard and Margaret. So cherish baby Beth, just as each of you were a blessing to our family on your first Christmas, she blesses this Christmas.'" Then Mother added, reading from the card, "And thank you very much for the cookies. It's signed, Santa Claus."

Everyone laughed and applauded when Mother finished reading. Then Father said, "Well, Beth's too small to hand out gifts, so Bruce, it's still your job this year."

The phonograph record had come to the end of "Come All Ye Faithful," and Father went to put on another record. My memory fades with that image.

Seventy years later I take into my hand the Santa Christmas card which was found in a box of photos after Mother died. The Santa image is old fashioned, his red suit faded.

Inside is Santa's message about children at Christmas. The writing is in my mother's clear, careful hand.

THE LAST CHRISTMAS

I was angry. A month before my sixteenth birthday, walking head down into the cold and blowing snow, I felt trivial. It was that confused state of adolescence about identity that has no guide posts. No one understood me. No one understood that the experiments I was doing in my basement lab might someday prove important. I was trying to concoct a salve to relieve the eczema and impetigo that had plagued me since early childhood. When I went to a doctor about the infected impetigo he applied gentian violet on my face, making me look like an aborigine. I refused to go to school looking like that. I was in my lab hoping to find something in nature that would cure eczema. That night my dad yelled at me while I was working with a chlorophyll solution I had created. I had been turning on the faucet as I needed water. Dad accused me of not caring that he and Mom were trying to go to sleep, and that the pipes pounded when I turned the faucet on and off. I hadn't heard that noise. I hadn't at first even heard the thumping on the floor overhead when my dad was stomping in anger. Then he came to the cellar door and shouted, "Dammit, Bruce, stop that noise. Don't you know its eleven o'clock?"

Confused by his anger and my own I retreated. I slammed the back door hard as I could as I went out into the moonless, overcast night. Now they'd know they were being unfair. The newly fallen snow made that dry, squeaky sound under my overshoes as I walked, then ran until the cold air began to hurt my lungs. It was Christmas week. Pearl Harbor had been attacked two weeks earlier. Night-time temperatures had been below freezing all week but no one talked about weather. At the family dinner table the only topic was about when my brother Richard would be going off to war. They talked about who among his college friends had already volunteered. Mother's eyes got watery as she reached over and took Richie's hand.

"Two years from now and you'll probably be drafted " Rich said to me, "unless you volunteer sooner. The navy will take you at seventeen."

He was joking because he knew very well that I was only half way through my junior year of high school. And now what kind of future was it going to be for all of us? Everyone knew it was going to be a long war. I knew then that as soon as I was out of high school I would be drafted and not go to college to study biology. The war had made every thing uncertain. No one in my family had done any shopping for the holidays since December 7th.

I felt guilty for making my father angry. Being angry and sorry at the same time made me mad, as if it were only my fault. I hadn't wanted to annoy my parents. I had been concentrating on a green solution as it turned a deeper color in the Erlenmeyer flask. I had ordered that flask from Scientific Supply and got in the mail the day after Pearl Harbor. It made my lab look professional.

The experiment seemed to be working the way I had hoped. It was a serious experiment, just like in a real laboratory. The extracts I had made during the summer from several different tree leaves were being mixed in different concentrations. When I mixed the chlorophyll residue with zinc oxide ointment and spread it on the rash on my arms it seemed to help more than when I just used the ointment alone. When dad came and yelled at me, I was concentrating on the boiling solution and had no thought of anyone upstairs.

As I hurried away from the house I imagined that my running off like that would give my folks something to worry about. The temperature was below freezing and there was a wind from the north. Now, I thought, let them worry. It was their fault too. But I felt confused. There wasn't a name for it. Anger was only a part of it. It was like having a deep empty feeling and not knowing anything.

I hardly noticed the cold as I hurried toward downtown, drawn there by the familiar light reflected on the low hanging clouds racing before the wind. Downtown was where we kids hung out after school, like at the Chocolate Shoppe. I was running and then walking and kicking at the snow. I was breathless after ten blocks. A steady north breeze burned my cheeks.

When I reached the business section, I stepped out of the wind into the entryway of Shriver Johnson department store. To me this store was a grand emporium, especially during Christmas season when mother would take me, only me, on a shopping trip. There would be carols playing through loudspeakers. Little change boxes would shoot up wires to a cashier in the balcony. Pillars were hung with large bells or candy canes. Crowds of people would be shopping. It was always a happy place.

I was breathing hard and had to rest. I noticed then that there were few cars moving on Phillips Avenue, and I hadn't seen any people walking. I was brought back to the season, the Christmas season, when I noticed what was in the display windows. A cardboard Santa Claus figure was holding a placard offering discounts on women's wear. A red banner with white lettering was draped across the backdrop proclaiming "Peace on Earth, Good Will Toward Man." I wondered if the store might take it down now that Christmas was ruined. Next to Santa was an artificial Christmas tree, its colored lights blinking off and on. It was past eleven at night and there was no one downtown in Sioux Falls at that hour to enjoy holiday lights. They no longer seemed cheerful. It wasn't as pretty as the way Christmas trees had always been before.

On the inside corner of the display window a manikin in a long black holiday dress had her skirt pulled to mid-thigh. A placard offered "Silk hosiery - $1.75 pair while they last," over which was scrawled in red ink, "Sold Out." The manikin's long legs reminded me of those of our roomer Dorothy in her bathrobe. I nearly bumped into her last week as she came out of the bathroom next to Rich's and my bedroom. Dorothy was a student at Augustana College and rented the spare room at the front of the house, "to help pay the rent," mother explained. Dorothy had been with us since September, coming and going. She was pleasant, but too busy to be a part of our family life. She was very pretty. I thought about her body. A lot. I imagined her naked body and felt guilty. Lust. Reverend Olson preached about lust. Thinking those thoughts was as bad as committing real adultery. That seemed nuts, because that meant all my buddies were sinning every day.

As she came out of the bathroom, towel wrapped around her head and in a hurry, her robe had opened and I got a glimpse of most of her legs. She had smiled at me as she passed in the hallway. I wondered what it would be like to hold her. Those feeling I had about Dorothy were steeped in loneliness and an empty longing.

Out of the wind but feeling the cold penetrate my cloth coat through its thin sheepskin lining I began to shiver. I realized about then how dumb it had been to come downtown. It was stupid to blow up like I had. Anger was making Christmas week all the more bleak. Christmas had always been happy because there would be toys. One year I got a wood-burning pen that I used to make plaques for a Boy Scout project. Then there was the year I had been given microscope with slides of insect wings. I still had it in my lab.

Christmas meant excitement, like the anxious anticipation of Christmas morning and seeing the family's light-filled tree for the first time. We use to line up in the order of our ages, the youngest first to descend the stairs. We thrilled at seeing the tree lights, that radiance of the moment which we shared together. It was an old family tradition.

A voice behind me broke into my reverie. The words came slowly as if the speaker was being careful not to startle me.

"Kinda cold to be out, isn't it?" The man's voice was just a bit louder than a whisper.

I turned to face Mr. Albert, the night policeman all of us kids knew. He was never the tough cop, but we knew that he could be firm if we cut up too much on Phillips Avenue after school.

"Oh, hi Mr. Albert."

"You're Mr. Thorson's boy, aren't you."

"Yes, sir. I'm Bruce. "

"Well, son, it's a bit past curfew for kids, so I wondered what brought you down here."

"Oh, nothing. Nothing important anyway."

"Folks know you're downtown?"

"No. They're mad a me so I just went for a walk."

Mr. Albert's voice changed to that quiet but firm tone.

"Well Bruce, it's now past midnight and we better get you home."

"I can walk home okay," I said, guessing that if Mr. Albert took me home in the patrol car I would get there before I was ready to face my parents.

"Sure," Mr. Albert said, "but you'll just make your parents worry that much longer."

I hoped that they were worried.

"Well, hop in the cruiser and we'll get you home in a jiffy."

The car was stifling hot. There was the smell of tobacco and food, probably tuna fish, I thought. The sooner he got me home the better, even if I was going to catch it from the folks. We rode in silence out of the business district and south into the darker residential neighborhoods. I felt like a little kid. It was a lonely feeling, as if I hadn't grown up yet.

As we moved down the street slowly, I saw for the first time that night houses with lighted wreaths in the windows. Christmas trees seem to glow from inside several of the houses. The warmth radiating from those rooms made the holiday seem as if nothing had changed and Christmas would be like it always had been. People were pretending the season was the same as always. But this year wasn't like any of the holidays I had known all the years of my life. A child was safe in the midst of his family. My parents made Christmas for the kids. It was a celebration of being together. Now Rich would be going to war.

"You'll have to point out which house 'cause I'm not quite sure where you live."

"It's the second one from the end. The one with the porch light on," I told him

The porch light meant trouble because it was seldom turned on. It was like an angry light.

"Now, you take care, son, and have a Merry Christmas," Mr. Albert said, leaning over to pat me on the shoulder as I turned to get out the open car door.

"You too, Mr. Albert," I said, trying to be cheerful but my voice was strained. I wasn't ready to go into the house but the patrol car remained at the curb, waiting for me to go in.

Once in the entryway where a dim night

light burned from an outlet near the floor, I kicked off my overshoes. The door to Dorothy's room was just to the left off the entry, convenient for her to come and go without disturbing the family. I wondered if she was in her room but there was no light under the door. But where she was didn't seem very important at that moment. I was steeling myself for father storming down the stairs. I was rehearsing how I would tell him I was sorry.

Rich's and my bedroom was at the back of the house, down a short hallway beyond the dining room and kitchen. I wasn't sneaking, but walked quietly, careful not to run into the reading lamp next to dad's easy chair. The Christmas tree in the living room was centered on the bay window. It was unlit. There was no sound from upstairs. I passed the staircase and still heard nothing. The house was still, as if no one was at home. As I went through the kitchen I could see light shining from under our bedroom door. It hadn't occurred to me that my dad might be waiting there.

I opened the door slowly to find Rich in his own bed, a blanket pulled over his head. I eased the door closed. The light switch was just left of the doorway and I quickly turned it off. I undressed to my underwear and slipped under the covers of my bed.

In the dark Rich's voice was muffled by his blanket.

"Mom said to remind you that you promised to work at Mr. Moses store tomorrow. She'll wake you up at six."

I lay on my back, unable to sleep. Nothing had happened. There had been no scolding. No lecture. I couldn't figure it out. A chill passed through me, as if the cold from the wind had followed me to bed. The pretend was over. The magic was over of imagining a *nisse* might live hidden in our house, or that a Santa Clause really did eat the cookies and drank the milk set out Christmas Eve. Hearing the Bible story always made me think there had been a golden aura around the baby in a rough feed trough, there among ordinary creatures of the earth. I wanted that picture to be true. The words promised a peaceful world in which wise men were real. But that night I thought they were just a part of an old story told over and over again but just made up.

I fell into a deep sleep. It was the smell of bacon that awakened my consciousness before Mom knocked softly on the door and announced that it was ten to six. Rich grunted and rolled over without saying a word as I got dressed.

I worked Wednesday and Thursday at Mosie's neighborhood grocery, ten hours altogether. I was paid ten dollars, plus a two dollar "Christmas Bonus." Mr. Mosies said I should use my money for presents, because, as he said, it was the season of giving. I did go downtown on Friday, Christmas Eve day, and bought bright woolen socks for Beth and Ellie. For Rich I got a pair of heavy wool socks he could use with boots. I wrapped all three presents and put them under the tree. The wall bookcase I had made in shop at school I had hidden in the basement. Christmas morning I would bring it up for Mom and Dad when we opened gifts.

Christmas Eve day no one mentioned anything about my leaving the house Tuesday night. It might not have happened as far as anyone was concerned. Even my Dad didn't mention it. He was home from his traveling job and helping in the kitchen with

Christmas Eve dinner. He was actually nice to me. It seemed even kind of funny to me that he had to tell us, as he did every Christmas, that in Norway they didn't decorate their houses with wreaths at Yule because wreaths were just for funerals.

Christmas Eve Dad had all of us gather in the living room to listen to President Roosevelt's radio talk. Our tree lights glowed red and green, their reflection in the front window duplicating the tree. The packages beneath the branches were colorful. The pine spell was nice.

The whole world was in a struggle, the President said, to keep our freedom. His voice sounded strong when he said everyone would have to sacrifice.

Christmas morning the family had breakfast together before opening presents. It wasn't often that we all had breakfast together anymore like we once did when we were little. We listened to the news on the radio. Pearl Harbor was still frantically dealing with the wounded and the burning ships and buildings. The Japanese had invaded the Philippines and were threatening Manila.

We all gathered in the living room after breakfast to open gifts. Since Beth was the youngest, she would distribute the gifts, as had always been the family tradition. It seemed strange to me that we were hanging on to that old tradition. Maybe the oldest person should pass out the gifts. That would be my Dad.

I hadn't gone to the basement and the lab during the week. Right then it seemed kind of dumb to be imagining I was going to be some kind of scientist. I wanted to tell my parents I was sorry for Tuesday night, but there never seemed to be a proper time. But they did like the little bookcase after I brought it up from the basement. Mom thanked me for doing a nice job. After that I opened my gifts. A plain tan shirt and a leather belt was the gift from the folks. Rich gave me a copy of *Science* magazine and a card saying I would get a year's subscription.

Everyone laughed at the bright sox when the girls opened their gifts. But it still didn't seem like Christmas to me. It was a lot more serious that it had been when I was little. I felt none of the excitement I had felt when I was eight and got an electric train.

And it wasn't even a Lionel. That afternoon while I read my magazine I began to understand that Christmas was not just about getting play things. Maybe it was mostly about people trying to be nice. To show love, I guess.

※

About the Author

Author of a detective/mystery novel *The Albino Stag Witness*, self-published in the spring of 2002 with iUniverse, Robert Feragen first published five of the six short stories in this edition with his own Cripple Grackle Press. That limited edition for family and friends and was entitled "Dakota Christmases Remembered" It was printed with a computer printer and then bound by the author. The current edition has been renamed "July's Christmas Doll" to feature one of the six short stories. The subtitle retains the original title.

Writing these stories the author took himself on a sentimental journey back to Christmas seasons of the 1930's when the reality of the Great Depression made gift giving modest but did not diminish his family's enthusiastic embracing of the spirit of the season. Being fictionalized accounts of the author's experiences while growing up in North and South Dakota, these stories recount conflicts, joys and personal discoveries realized during the holiday season.

A graduate of the Iowa Writers' Workshop in 1952, Feragen taught English at Texas A & M and the State University of New York at Plattsburgh for a total nine years before starting a twenty-eight year career in the rural electric and public power industries. In 1978 President Jimmy Carter appointed him Administrator of the Rural Electrification Administration where he served until January, 1981. Returning to South Dakota he was employed by East River Electric Power Cooperative as Manager of Administrative Services until 1986 when he was made General Manager of the cooperative.

Feragen retired in 1990. He and his wife of sixty-three years, Madlin Ann Melrose Feragen, traveled throughout the United States and Mexico, lived in Rockport, Texas, for ten years and returned to South Dakota to live in Sioux Falls. During his retirement he has continued to write poetry and short fiction, some of which has been published by regional media. Feragen celebrated his eighty-eighth birthday in January, 2013.

Made in the USA
Charleston, SC
23 October 2013